BECAUSE

OF A

WOMAN

Malanda Jean-Claude

More information at www.ogjean.com

Cover illustration by Bobby Rogers and Jared Tuttle

Layout and design by Lewis Mundt

Editing by Lewis Mundt and Kels Brunn-Bryant

ISBN: 978-0-9966750-0-0

First Edition: August 2015

10 9 8 7 6 5 4 3 2 1

CONTENTS

INTRODUCTION 5

ACT I: CHASING WINDS 9

YEAR OF THE DRAGON........................ 70

ACT II: THE BLUES... 82

PART II... 106

PART III.. 138

ACT III: FORBIDDEN FRUITS........................... 150

ACT IV: SOUL WIND...................................... 172

ABOUT THE AUTHOR 189

to my mother,

i have seen moons dance across your teeth
and suns awakened by your energy solo, this is
for you.

this is for the pain you've felt.

to my father, *shalom*.

to my siblings, i live through your laugh.

thank you for air.

INTRODUCTION

Even when your words don't feel like magic to you anymore, keep writing. They are magic to someone else and at some point they always return for you to feel them again.

No man believes water exists until he drinks from his own skin. we, people of this realm who occupy breathing space and a body, exist solely on a belief system of tangibility and proof. how we got here is the human question, how we travel is the soul wandering. if i highlighted my affairs with the moon and fornication with a flower nymph, or perhaps; if you follow closely every leaf engraved with detail on these pages you turn, i may very well suffice the bias in your belief and convince you that i was kissed by a deity. the garden woman, the second coming of billie holiday head wrapped with flowered thoughts.

i am no stranger to controversy and autumn. i find peace in changing colors and falling in arms of women still learning to hold newborns correctly. i am the result of that kiss. the moment butterflies make love faintly beneath concrete and find a rose grew from those cracks. you and i both are the caterpillars. in transition, i came to this conclusion that heaven is a thing of the mind my friends. we are beings of vibration and resistance; moderation is our new home. choice is exactly what it is— just another place to choose from, and instincts often correspond better when parallel to new introductions. one must first understand option in order to make choice otherwise the blind picks. but let me help you by saying this; nothing is final until it is, and even then; growing pains become defiant and we begin to doubt ourselves. we grow tired and go wrong but we learn. we lose, we cry, we lose again, scream, we come home and find shape into being. this is how people are made. this is metamorphosis; the birthright in the ability we all have to spring back into shape. i know growth divulges pain and reality misuses breath, but slow it down. become familiar with infinity and read completely open in acceptance for the mind.

as usual, time unveils precision and you may find god being closer than your truth. i am nothing more than what you think your fingers can touch yet i hold everything you have led your mind to believe i am. therefore, i am. i have seen mothers bare children in backseats with hallow prayer for every push, babies cry their first war but they live. they breathe for they too understand struggle and secrets buried underneath the village of a mother's tongue and a wise man saying, *you should listen more.* i am the child-state of ears in adolescent molding into understanding but i cannot be grabbed. today, what i cherish most is knowing that i share last names with the wind and cradle honor of mothers natal by the same sun. i have learned to become a sponge and absorb where i can with whatever life gives, so i try not downplay how distant we all are. there comes a point in life when appetite becomes more than just a taste of tongue and hunger is no longer a cry for the body to be filled with diet but a longing for intimacy as a spiritual connection, and this, this is where you are.

follow each page with an open mind and trust your bones by intuition that beauty still lives, and all you have to do is reach for it. i am not here to mock what you've held to be true— i only have one conviction. that is to fill your conscience with light; unclutter space to help you see magic in all things that have been.

ACT I: CHASING WINDS

V ulnerability is the hardest emotion to conquer as anyone. honesty comes easy when surrounded by four walls but once the curtains drop, we shame the essence of being naked in front of everyone because we have yet to conquer that instinctive nature of ourselves. being exposed can make anyone feel frail in their own body and some even grow defenseless because of the fact. it's scary— i get it. nobody finds pleasure in being stripped and cut open for the world, but wounds are so necessary.

although it is threatening having to be cautious in your own skin, and certainly a lot easier to stay closed off than being an open bottle. we grow in increments. we shift the energy of fear when we confront ourselves with truth, total nakedness, and i've yet to find anything more liberating next to love than vulnerability. with exposure there is potential harm, but in transparency there is safety too. nature's camouflage— predators pass you because they have nothing to attack. vulnerability is the only bridge to real connection, the raw stuff.

when building trust you must lose the connotation of exposure as weak.

we live in a society where emotions are placed on a scale of masculinity weighed against what it means to be woman. delicate, compassionate— sensitive to nature's time clock. men are short handed for wearing empathy as a wristwatch, and women oppressed for being themselves while everybody gets crucified. censored by the gatekeepers for swimming above the status quo, to break free from the glass ceiling designed to diminish complexity. i can only speak of certainty as a man of unfiltered emotions, and only as a passenger observing the nature of my counterpart. vulnerability is a hard thing for a man. not to downplay what any woman has gone through when given measure of how, when or where they can speak without judgment, but society is designed to keep women subdued and men robotic. we have to break loose from these barriers for the sake of survival. we are taught that to be male is to be stoic and militant, while a woman is to be submissive and elastic to the needs of men; something to bend as we see fit. soon after conformity we grow disoriented even with the sense of ourselves. we lose touch and begin to scrap for understanding of which emotions are allowed for expression and which cannot.

as we get older, the very things we were punished for become a prison most of us will fail to evolve, and i blame habituation for that. i have always thought about the choice of man—as a people the responsibility to choose is heavy for any living mortal. in fact, it is our greatest freedom and our biggest downfall. nothing is easy but life is beautiful this way. i urge you to take the risk of being cut open in exchange for new air and feel more than just blood in your skin. choose to live a life of liberation and not breathe under control of anyone. be unguarded with how you choose to unveil and secure those beliefs as if no one else's matter, then respect your differences. understand how you operate internal before you offer yourself to someone— people give slow handshakes, watch for hidden fallacies of their own faults. play your heart safe.

life is a course of surveillance and you come to find that things people bash you for are often parallel to those they lack in themselves. they envy you for being able to carry their void with such conviction and a light spirit. trust me, having the ability to sense your own emotions and pour them with dignity is much more redemptive than a body in distress. there is nothing flattering about numbness. the moment you make covenant with your body and accept the liberty to feel and experience all emotion without apology, you will thank yourself in a love letter. which brings me to my next point; why do people run from the fate of feeling their own sentiments? simple— people run from the pain of knowing, the notion of ignorance being bliss is a lot easier to swallow than the suffering of truth. it is a lot like dreaming, the sudden rush of adrenaline as a way to escape a nightmare when everything in your body is warning you to wake up. the pain of having to deal with the aftershock makes you want to forget, but do not panic. emotions exist to remind our bodies that divinity is in arm's reach. it arouses awareness and serves poetry for our bones to keep alive. your veins to be faucet and pump more than just water, so give yourself permission to 'feel' more. feel beyond what you think you know and even further past your comfort level because that my friends— is absolute freedom. never quiet your desire for infinity.

be patient with me,

i'm learning to project what i feel better.

emotions are fluid and sometimes breed sense

i mistake the universe for understanding

and forget my mind was not made for convincing.

i am infinite.

way too often i forget

we are not distant relatives— i do not blame you for the mix.

i am in the process of rearranging family portraits

in making room for a home.

sometimes i mistake heaven for staircases.

— gold frame.

the gift of being passionate is that you feel everything,
the curse is that sometimes you feel too much.

— berakah/sword.

i've always wanted to be somebody's first.

first line

first pain

first gun

first bang,

explosion.

first love

first everything that changed what was.

have you been moved by the winds lately?

or have you forgotten you're an earthquake

learning to open at the mouth

with more prayer— less noise, *conviction*

and still get your point across.

— somebody's first.

moments come when the wind blows

and the ghost of you not being here

still haunts the thoughts of where you might be now,

you moved our home someplace else.

my bones left empty,

my blood in rage.

heart chaotic.

mouth, still learning to forgive

but i've grown skin

and enough water to not forget

how to nurture the garden of what you once were.

astral girl,

i always knew our tongues connected

but our taste buds gave in to the moon different.

do not apologize for not remembering.

i found forgiveness in the things you forgot.

— **chicago winds.**

the heart is the most delicate,

most profound muscle of memory next to touch.

being in a space where love sprouted

my heart stuttered nervous to every *bone.*

goose bumps claimed home to every pore

and truth is

i never stopped being in love with the place.

the smile

the wind

the people,

the aura kept bottled in ocean shores.

i believed once wine bottles only made love to
strangers in paris but they live in the city.

nwoke, a foreign name.

tomorrow.

i'll sit face to face with the universe

intimate and kiss her garden flowers.

trace her lifelines with watermarks and bury my
blueprint wrapped in blankets under arm.

stay.

i've always thought our first time this way.

you, still. motionless.

a zipper away from being naked in vulnerability, and
me.

well, i just am.

a nomad.

still chasing the moon in your smile.

p.s,

your dimples left an impression on me.

— **15th street/blue trains.**

do you love me?

do you love me..

do you love me?

said the sun to the moon.

one of many letters part 4

the wind always calmed when i wrote about you, i..
woke up promptly at 2:59 to prepare my tools. 1 pen,
2 journals, open window, streets— *silent.*

i'd close my eyes to find you behind the curl of my
lashes you slept next to my stigmatism.

eyes bloodshot in a sober woman

love, you, yes you with the words of gods in olympia.

women craved your metaphors

but i craved your laugh.

a laugh like thunder, you were a man in so many ways

and i was woman enough to show you how to love a
woman enough.

is it insane that you didn't need to speak with me
when you laid next to my silhouette.

'love, why are you screaming?'

why do fools fall in love?

because fools are people too.

cigarette smoke inhaled, love exhaled. carbon.

elements of the periodic table were more tangible
than time, she no longer used the night for sleeping.

exhausted only when words seemed lazy,
encompassing his entirety.

under anatomy, flesh and veins, i found you dancing
in my blood stream.

hesitation to fall in love with things yet touched,

i free fell into you like the freed prisoner i was.

you chose me,

your soul asked mine to lay seeds in the garden of
eden,

you dug deeper into mine.

deep in pink matter, garden wetter than licked lips.

cigarettes lit to bring distortion to the pretty picture,
see..

king, you didn't how beautiful you were.

how beautiful you are,

you. painted landscapes inside of me—

thick paintbrushes and white residue.

valleys, oceans, and streams were your specialty.

how many women had a picasso?

you, never answered that question.

they can take pieces of you. pieces that would never
be mine i knew you weren't for sale, i just…

wanted to be the object of your metaphors.

i'm a selfish woman.

i wanted love to choose us,

to impregnate you with sweet thoughts of me.

i wanted to be the drug you injected daily.

the melanin in your lungs.

asthma formed in the back of my throat when i said
your name.

baby —

why do you love the girls who can't pronounce your name?

your heart was too big for comfort.

then again, you weren't in the business of making me 'comfortable'

you wanted honesty, i gave that.

deposits i prayed you wouldn't withdraw,

checking balance like checkbooks, i wanted your signature to spell my name.

i wanted to be selfish with you, to wrap my legs around you and use every ounce of energy you could pray for.

your stamina was written inside of me like the stretch marks that kissed the ass of a real woman.

i do not wish to be indecisive,

my ribcage is more miracle than it does hold lung.

i have a childlike heart about the world most days

but today

i just wanted to hear from you.

do you love me?

i want to take the collar into the nearest room and
remove the buttons of the heart you say has a hard
time expressing love.

astral girl.

i like honesty.

it

turns

me

on.

then i'll never lie.

you thank me,

why?

because.

do you say thank you to your reflection for showing

you your face?

exactly.

i feel connected.

my mind walks on water whenever we speak,

my soul embodies a spirit of everything you are

your essence is a tongue dance i have kept secret in
light of bystanders.

selfish, forgive me for a mouthful.

i was never good at sunday dinners or

greetings for the round table, but love

can you stay awhile?

love me through dessert.

admire from afar *but* do not mutilate me.

i become wind at the knife of a heart surgeon

scary,

do not let my mystery escape me from you.

marvel without guard

touch, me.

rigid, nature comprehends my morning salute.

be water. be holy. fish me into understanding.

cram what you know, *teach me.*

do not, anatomize.

only touch what you crave— your hands are
breathing.

be wind

be sharp

be knife

be water

breathe yourself in my ribcage.

convince stardust in bare skeletons you belong next
to my immortal.

love,

can you hang with the holy in my bones?

yes.

no?

time has a pulse,

i'll wait.

— ethereal.

we fear rejection but i am not one to throw curiosity
to the wolves if you breathe with good intentions.
foolish. the sedation of love often never make sense,
but i am here respectfully. i would honor the distance
before i find myself on a run from something i didn't
even try to understand.

one of many letters: untitled.

you radiate peace, your aura is fascinating.

your laugh is most infectious, a sound my ears have never heard.

i listen to your soul and become aroused with life.

no one has been able to inject electricity in my veins like you have.

you teach love without restriction and the patience of loving someone who needs *time* to know.

you allow me to embrace the existence of who i am without limit or boundary.

i experience freedom with you, and that, is a piece of heaven on a plate *truly.*

and the most important of all things,

you love yourself.

these are seven things i admire about you.

we like tumbling.

wrestling too.

you were the greatest sparring partner i've ever had

that is truth.

your heart is a home to someone else but nirvana to me.

paradise.

9: twenty-one, morning.

i'm going to take some time away and make sure i'm good. you have taught me a lot about being 'here' but i will not, nor be comfortable with feeling like a secret lover to you. i have an obligation to get what i deserve— i put so much love in effort to breathe for the both of us. i've been an outstanding woman, but i will not compete nor beg you to validate me. you have your ways but they do not work for me. so if you need, or enjoy the eyes and hearts of multitudes, i can't give you that. and i won't feel any less than because you allow it. i love you, i always will. absolutely in love with you, but i deserve better in that department. i'm done blaming my insecurities for things that most women would not tolerate either. you are free to love, king. i have no animosity towards you but i do deserve a man that craves one woman, me. and it is not my job to demand that from you.

love,

astral girl.

9: fifty-six, rising.

thank you for many lessons. my instincts now recognize an art form only flowers have mastered and i am grateful to see. being open has never been easy. thank you for not running though you had every reason to form back into wind. you offered glory in ways i can never dishonor, ways even you, never understood. i know my heart is stubborn. hesitant and often scared in any face of commitment— your patience is a festival. i acknowledge the nights we spent in silence and everything your aura made love to. this is your decision, i won't fight it this time. i want nothing but ideal for you and it's rare that you ever miss— *you hit the bullseye.* may you never compromise for your heart deserves better than that. never settle for being shorthanded, nobody wins this way. i am sorry. i wish i could give you enough reason to wait for a heart, but i loved you with everything i knew how. be fortunate, be full, be peaceful as i pray the woman inside you learns to forgive. sadly

everything is courted with expiration dates— this is
that. i really don't believe in breaks, love. nothing ever
comes back the same. i'm not up for playing in
fragments of what you leave behind only to watch
you not come back at all. i just won't, nor am i willing
to go through that but please do find love in yourself,
queen.

sincerely,

man on the moon.

2 days later.

this is hell for me.

yeah. but…hey

wow. okay.

what do you want me to say?

nothing that you don't naturally feel.

if 'yeah..but hey' is all you have left i'll take it just as i did when you first hinted on the word dearest.

all is good.

you know how i feel about
space. i don't believe in that.
i never have, nor do i plan
to. not anytime soon, not
with you.

love.

you left.

you didn't secure me like i needed to, i had no other
option. i needed you to make me a priority and you
wouldn't do that. i pleaded with you. i asked many
times to help me validate whatever it was we were
entering together. you wouldn't. you chose your
audience over me and it's hard to recover from that.
i'd give my last breath but you refuse to hear me. i felt
like your secret and i couldn't bare it anymore. just
know i loved you, *remember why i did.*

okay.

i hear you.

i hear you.

whatever man.

i'm not doing this with you.

stop.

i plan to.

stop saying things you don't
mean. stop taunting yourself
with winded emotions. you
say these things then you
run when it all gets too real.
we can just stop here. you
won't hear from me
anymore and i'm certain that
i won't hear from you either.

bye.

stop telling me what to do! how to feel! there is nothing wrong with how i communicate. i didn't ask you for much, at all. i was patient with you and never had other motives. how difficult would it have been to reassure me of who i was and where i stood. it was overwhelming to be opened to your fan base, and instead of telling me how to deal with them, you should have made sure that i was good first. you didn't and you refuse to own up to that. but after all, i'll respect your space. peace.

i called you..

but i guess you blocked me.

i get it.

i am good at pretending that i am doing well.

i've had to for survival, i'd rather write instead.

i know a million thoughts will fall

and separation will feel like hell for nights my body
will grow amnesia,

please bring me a pen. serve me gentle.

i would rather spill on paper.

i have wounds only ink would understand.

— **pain.**

love.

leave me alone.

bye.

---

last thing i swear.

'lauryn hill x sweetest thing'

ears.

i know this gets confusing and stressful and i know

we have so much to learn but i'm willing to learn,

with you. i want you to feel safe, with me.

— bipolar love.

argument part 1: a call for home

how does this not tear your soul out your chest?
explain to me how it doesn't still haunt you. i see you
when i sleep. i miss you when i'm happy, i smile when
i'm sad. i get lost in memories of warmth that's never
touched my hands and i get angry that i haven't been
able to trust another soul like i trusted you.

'come back to me' and you never come.

'hold me' and i'm still cold.

'kiss me' and my lips grow numb.

my soul aches for you even when my mind is less
awake when it does.

i never want another woman to touch you.

the fact that your words aren't for me anymore still
hurt.

you should be home. you always miss dinner now.

you were never supposed to leave.

i was never supposed to let you *leave*.

argument part 2: in reflection of home.

i know the feeling all too well.

you come up in days more than i like to admit.

i'm sorry my arms don't stretch anymore.

i still visit the sanctuary i built in bare hands with you.

i close fist and pray you peace on sunday mornings
but my heart is heavy and prayers don't travel with
chains like that.

instead. i leave silent notes in bookmarks hoping you
visit and engulf in moments time stroked against us
and became anything but close.

you nod some days. you smile because i touch you
without permission but my wind familiar. i know
what it's like to feel all you describe, love.

i still crave you at 2am. those were our peak hours.

we never really slept much, and truth is, i missed you
for months and i still do. i hate that you're not here
much anymore.

we were supposed to be good.

'you'll be strong' you'd always say.

where is home now?

i will go through life with part of my heart forever silently crying. there will be parts of my soul no man will ever understand why he can't go. and when you fall in love again, i will weep for hours and hours, and find happiness only when the last tear had fled my body. you will drain everything from me slowly, and i am blessed to ache for such a man. remember me in your spare time and hold my hand on special occasions. there will forever be a soul in this universe who loves, loved, and will forever love you more than any other woman ever could. i don't know why we do this, spoken emotions layered beneath empty solution. we have no relief. i have no hope for us again, i will lie in this bed of thorns, more silently as i become accustomed to the sharpness. and you will grow and love and move away, and i may do the same. and on your wedding day, before you say 'i do', think of my smile, my laugh, the curve of my back, and kiss her with conviction. i will clap for you.
i will always, clap for you.
your biggest fan.

— wedding day/her last letter.

i wanted to meet the women who inspired you and kiss their foreheads. each cheek, and tell them i loved them. that they were beautiful. i will tell them about the wonders you've performed. you allowed me not to fall in love with your mind, but everything immortal and infinite. whatever woman you choose and see fit to allow in your space next, make sure her crown is adjusted. love her with conviction. you have the power to make any woman feel infinite, decorated, and that, is immaculate.

— **her last prayer.**

i'll go.

but *this.*

is not me walking or withholding resistance from you.

headaches after arguments.

these are the worst memories of nostalgia.

i'm going to finish crying, wipe my face, and smoke this cigarette.

— her last decision.

we got caught up in our differences that we lost sight of the magic this all was. what this is, or could've been. i asked for patience and you gave it freely. i never asked for love but you couldn't ignore the earthquake in your chest when my name came. you shook pride from under my feet and i took pleasure in being out of place. the turbulence of new grounds— i was a *fan,* it didn't hurt. i asked for a friend and you became three; lover, confidant, a reminder. i couldn't ask for more. i know men would go to war to find a space that i was. i'm lucky to have walked with you. your energy was surreal. you gave love unconditionally even on days i didn't deserve the seven moons you became. you cried not because you were weak, but because you felt a heaven in the chest for me. i will never belittle your effort to love me out loud. the intensity. the passion. the craving you became. i know it's bad karma to hurt good people and i don't want that. i hate being the one to add salt on old wounds so i won't come around anymore.

— **tug of war.**

she was an open wound and i kissed her with salt on my lips.

melancholy: *(n)*

1. the kind of sad you never find forgiveness for.

three: fourteen, her reach.

i'm out of place, but i miss you in ways that aren't friendly. and i'm not sure how to go about that.

i guess there's nothing to do but enjoy the feels and keep living. i just have this passion for you that gets turned on more frequently than turned off. i still crave you, and i know i shouldn't. i know you said you wanted my friendship only, and i respect that. but there's a woman in me who still desires to tangled white sheets and smooth legs wrapped around strong waists. i...wonder if you ever think of me that way. if you thought of me that way. can i confess something? i've always wanted to be kai. i remember your stories. i would listen to you read, and while tasting each syllable, i would desire to be the kind of woman who could make a man like yourself nervous. silly, i know. but honest. i'm rambling, i don't mind. do you? i used to think you were so sweet, you could've dipped your index finger in my tea and sufficed my need for honey. i have a way of romanticizing things i have never touched. you most likely get these texts often, women you've affected pouring their forms of poetic wooing into your space.

i hate feeling like a candidate for your heart and affections, but that's my own mental thing to filter out. i think i'll retire now. sleep is craving my cocoa butter kisses. you aren't required to respond, but you knew that. namaste, king.

nine: twenty-three, deflection.

to ramble is to search for freedom. uncontrolled
thoughts often remind me of a space i was, *lost*.
i admire anyone who can walk a thin line pushing
thresholds in a place like that.

chaos feeds the mind, it's an honor to still have a taste
of your mind travel.

vibrant.

raw.

honest.

unapologetic.

pure.

i want to love like that.

tell me something good, anything. i
need it with life right now…

remember the night i read my poetry to you, it was a
late night for us, up until the wee hours. i told you i
was in love with your energy and you felt it wrap you
into a safety net. you slept so peacefully, you told me
you thought i was laying right next to you. the night i
told you i saw you on the moon. you were and will
always be the majestic man on the moon. and i will
forever love you for giving me the gift of 'now' of
'being here.' never had i ever felt so secure in
someone. your words could cause the tower of jericho
to fall again. you still awaken cocoons inside my soul
and i thank you for those butterflies. they carry me far
in your recent absence. you divine being. i thank you.

— things i thought she forgot.

i came, i left. i came and it began to rain outside, your eyes began to swell with passionate clear water. 'how could i leave him' i thought. she was wise, she knew better than to be consumed by titles or expectations for tomorrow, she was a woman who wanted now. when i say i wanted you, i didn't want your promises, i wanted you at that moment, exactly how i needed you. maybe, had i articulated my desires better, i would still be tangled in those white sheets you fed me in. i...i didn't want to own you, nor be captive for you, nor scare you. nor consume you, did i say that already? let me reiterate. i wanted you when i wanted you. in my favorite coffee mug, i wanted to sip you into the mornings. to see your reflection in my hazelnut. i craved you, and fear you. no, not *you*, but you intimated me until this morning. foolish? to fear your reflection. you are water my king. i apologize, not 'my,' but king you still are and forever will be. i will always have passion and a burning flame in the back of my eyes for you. the stranger i fell in love with. i can still feel your kisses, and the bruises on my lips from the passion of your biting, remind me you were the only dream i'll ever remember.

— the last i actually heard from her.

your energy is close, i can still feel you.

not in the open

but you will live through every thought.

i will smile at the smell of leftovers with coffee you brewed every morning for a man who was not yet ready to love, be given or take a heart without question.

in memory of empty spaces, we built walls from broken ribs. i never knew why you wanted to be looked at so much.

tomorrow, when our days grow old and your voice is faint,

i will draw patterns to trace in trying to remember you.

i need to be sharp so don't be empty out of spite, not now. you can hate me tomorrow ~

and if i ask— may you lighten transition from intimacy to plain *friendship*. nobody should be thrown to the wolves like that.

signed,

man on the moon.

— acceptance.

most nights

she found addiction with a pen and slept under a
flame of a cigarette.

she bled on paper for a love neither

he, nor she knew how to raise proper

but they tried.

tried in ways they knew how.

she was not used to having withdrawals

but he left last night in exit of an argument,

one of their many breakups.

he missed her,

i. missed, her.

she missed him but both kept quiet—stubborn

this is how they were taught to love.

her tea would catch cold waiting in blankets

for better taste

but lonely is a friend of the night,

and nostalgia started to reek from tear stained sheets
tsunamis could not hold back under bridges anymore.

i had stories itching from the back of my throat

i wanted to come home,

i promise.

i was a rifle and my heart was at war,

but i did not want to come home to blood.

we exhausted everything.

friends now.

i'm sorry.

sorry that it took a few months and new people to
accept an apology.

forgive me.

— cigarette smoke.

i wrote about you for 4 months.

her last confession.

YEAR OF THE DRAGON

.

chasing the dragon.

the first time we spoke on the phone,

the moon fell. i remember my window clouded,
fogged with excitement of what our mouths would
say next,

our bodies nervous and unmoving. we sat there.

immersed in the ambiance of silence and a thousand
words, connection was inevitable.

we met in transition. you echoed my name first and
time stopped at the cue of tongue,

impatient.

moments bred in wild-flowers. i forgot to catch you a
rose and anticipation for more travel—curiosity
leeched on me.

aesthetics fluent, my ears fell.

thunder clashed with titans our minds fixated by
crossfire

war was the only time we kissed, shalom.

my mother gave warning to this kind of violence but
this

was the only time i wanted to kiss bullet wounds with
prayer on my lips.

sunflower:

so are you the charming type?

i don't think i'm charming actually. i speak my
thoughts and they come out as whatever people think
they are.

sunflower:

but you are. unknowingly i'm sure. which is probably
best anyway. your charming being unintentional
shows that it's a part of your character and not just an
act. i like it.

you can't fake passion. i think i like how intrigued you seem to be by my personality.

sunflower:

it's what i see. and i liked it from jump. you're much nicer than i expected you to be. if i can be completely honest i figured your persona would be more self-centered or standoffish. i shouldn't have pre-judged.

sometimes you can't help but to judge. it's another way of convincing the mind that it's not on its own.

sunflower:

don't let this be the last time i hear from you.

you'll hear my voice before i send you another text.

{CALL}

ring

ring

ring

ring

ring

ring

ring

ring

ring

ring

ring

why are you perfect?

sunflower:

that word. it's a wonderful compliment, and for that i thank you, yet it's hard to live up to. the feeling of being put on a pedestal as though i do no wrong— that'll destroy my conscience. however perfect to you or for you... i love everything about that because i find you provocative and that tempts me.

i believe perfection is measured in whatever you define it to be. in this case, the light you are. your soul is felt and i regard that energy as holy; a place without fault. the moment feels pure/relieved. perfect to me, not for me. i know expectation is a hot plate, and i have to learn how to feed proper even when drawn to the arousal of my own appetite, curiosity often gets the best of me— i'm still learning to pace myself but i believe we're all discolored in our own way.

nobody has it all but a flaw is subjective. *flawless* is the mind of a person who can determine the difference between a grape and a fruit, and admit the caterpillar has always been the butterfly. evolution is perfect. therefore, you are.

sunflower:

you have to excuse me, i often allow emotion or feelings i harbor for something to show in the ways i project them or react to things. it's more impulse than it is resistance, so please tell me if it starts to feel uncomfortable.

there's no discomfort where i live. i feel everything just as hard if not twice the same. what you've shown has proved to be more therapy than mind game. the energy is real—trust. i will take whatever you have to give.

sunflower:

i want to show you something.

what is it? show me.

sunflower:

my experiences within knowing a poet. what i've learned and gained. what i've given and basically telling times as they happen, in shape of how they happen. it's still unfinished but that is why you have to stay.

i can be patient.

i heard you fell asleep in class today.

you should get some rest.

sunflower:

what did i tell you last time? you couldn't keep me up
if i didn't let you. don't worry about that. i want to
stay.

i wanna talk to you. i like it when you stay up and
fight sleep for me. knowing the commitment behind
eyelids— the thought itself sedates my nature of
sacrifice. let me..

in that case, you just made my list of things to satisfy.

you awaken parts of me i never knew had gone to sleep.

ACT II: THE BLUES

Severe thunder and lightning just woke me up.

it would be amazing to roll over next to you.

— **her secret wish**

i don't like secrets,

i think

i'm

falling,

for you.

scared.

i don't like uncertainty and i can't package you, not even in boxes with open lids— i keep wanting to wear you like water.

bred in magic. at first glance my heart dropped.

gravity tumbled and time grew absent, weight.

vivid, a black and white photograph intrigued by a
shadow

inheritance,

love. i hear you come from a place of holy.

jazz in a rose garden—

i found wings carved in crevice of shoulder blades a
mouth can only reach with a wish and a prayer.

transcendence is an art form. may you remember
origin and carry moons in place of stardust.

if ever the feeling get too old, retrace back and…play.
remember my face in your coffee mugs.

today is your birthday, empress.

i pray serenity is a soft heart buried in soul for you.

here is mine.

— **first birthdays.**

twelve: fifty-nine

can i have you?

i'll take care of you. i've never been so close to someone inches away from perfection. my heart is floor painted with rose pedals.

have you ever been consumed by someone else's energy that nothing around you matters but them?

i want to be taken by you. doesn't matter where we go or what we do. take lead, i'll follow.

— first time she asked for a hand.

take what you need, love.

i'll continue to ask of you: please don't leave anytime soon.

if there's anything i know how to do, it's leave.

but you entice me.

you are a voice for souls who cannot find words. you speak what most people struggle to find an ear for. and i feel like you understand, you get it.

we all need someone who understands.

sunflower.

you just gave me a reason to exist more.

you have grown distant but i don't know how to hate
you.

— **a stretch.**

e n e r g y **shift.**

a woman can ask for space and miss you in the same sentence.

— a blind man's finding.

four: a.m.

i don't want to do this.

i haven't felt a weight on my heart this heavy in so long. you don't know how much you mean to me. i can't go to sleep like that.

five: a.m.

there was a sunrise and i captured it.

nine: a.m.

the sunrise was absolutely beautiful. that is how it was at the beginning of us.

— june.

i want to travel the world and make love in every country with you.

— june.

she had a laugh that made you want to believe in god.

lust.

to crave for someone deeply with intensity. a primal instinct to devour a portion where appetite is not crucified for wanting to breathe more.

guilt.

i've thought of everything your mouth can do wrapped around things with ability to erupt in places with suction.

sorry.

i shouldn't have said that.

let me touch you in places only i can write about.

i grabbed her by the throat but i didn't choke her. just kissed her so deep she forgot whose air she was breathing.

— **flower nymph.**

everybody is a poet when they think they're in love or find something that keeps them on edge.

i have a lot on my mind,

may i ask what's the matter

nothing is 'wrong.' i'm
just evolving and the
growth is intense.

what sparked this realization?

being alone.

sometimes growth
happens too fast for
me. i have to run to
catch up with myself.
like the old cliché
'alone in a crowded
room'

this is me.

alone as in having no

one to run to or being

the only person who

feels that way?

                              both in a sense,

                              but i haven't figured out yet..

i'm having a hard time comprehending. but what i can say is; do not fear change. you are evolving into what you are destined to become.

you are wise beyond your years and so you will outgrow a lot of things. you will have to catch up to the speed of your mindset. however, i do promise it is all a part of a greater plan.

you are teaching me patience.

breathe—

one day i'll fall in love with you like my ears did for hip-hop.

Part II

You preach constantly about my lack of effort to fix things, and when i try you get irritable. i never want to feel like a liability. many times i've walked out when you rather me sit but this is not new anymore. you hide too. i don't want to fight, but you know 'talk to you later' won't be for another day, and when i actually do reach you'll throb in anger to even entertain the demand of a conversation. we know this. i have no censor, and you have a temper. i won't even entertain the thought of maybes.

what do you want from me?

— questions that inch at the throat.

we lack consistency.

i want what i was
getting to know exactly
how it was.

i thought it was becoming one sided

so i backed off.

what?

---

i guess i know what
you meant now.

don't come at me with that.

are we talking or not.

this cycle is repetitive

i push every wrong
button with you. i hate
feeling like i have to
walk on eggshells to
have conversation with
you. i find venom at
the tip of tongue, and
worst yet, the silence
kills. if you really want
to know the truth, i
miss you— that won't
change for a while. but
in all honesty, i miss
the passion with less
cringe.

things got awkward for me. when i told you that i
loved you, it felt as though i was talking to a wall. not

that i required you to say it back or anything— i
would never ask you to lie for the sake of words not
to hurt, but if the feeling was mutual, why was it easy
for you to hold your tongue? i felt as though i made
you uncomfortable, and that was a hard feeling to
accept for someone you would fight the world for. i
was/am unsettled about talking with you again. i think
about that every time i talk to you.

i didn't say it back that
night because my love
was still building
though i already had it
for you. i wanted to
express it when it
reached a place where i
can scream it for the
world and have you
believe that i mean
every word, not just
because you said it to

me. i wanted you to 'feel' the weight of each passing letter through portals in which they came. the energy, the vibration in honest words. i wanted my emotions to travel with you, perhaps defy fear from holding breath. i wanted you to know i defeated any trace of uncertainty.

i believe in fairness of emotion as open letters and when the time come. i want to tell you everything in spite of wars i have kept hostage in question of my own tongue.

it was bittersweet for me.

and i'm sorry...

QUIET—

why do you do that?

i'm still here.

no. that's the thing.

you're not.

you keep saying that
you are

but it doesn't feel like
you anymore.

M,

i think of you so much it's almost sad. but i don't
want to begin conversation if i know i won't be able
to finish it because i have to get back to work. i know
how much you hate that.

> then balance, *baby.*
>
> you forget we survive
> off conversation with
> open letters.
>
> small talk isn't a thing
> for the mind and i
> don't want anything
> given with half
> interest. give me a
> spectrum or no colors
> at all. i get irritated
> when you drop a text
> and don't respond,
> especially when you

reach first.

i never got that.

but i know you have school—i promised to never get in the way of that.

just make sure you never forget me.

how could i?

i don't know. things happen to people. other people happen to people. i just ask that you don't forget about me.

i don't want to fight
anymore.

we stopped fighting a while ago, baby.

then come home.

narrator:

after that night, they didn't speak for a while.

sunflower:

i hope you've been speaking to me subliminally but if not, i do understand.

it's all been about you.

sunflower:

i know you don't like me right now, *M.*

but i am so sorry. i'm so much more attached than i thought i was. i don't know how that makes you feel, if someone being attached to you freaks you out— but i'm giving you honesty. i'm in this thing too deep. you still have a part of me but the thing is— i don't want it back. i just want to feel whole again...and that means i need you. *i need you.* i'm probably babbling right now and don't know when to end this text but it's been hell to get you to talk to me and now that i have, i just want to make sure you know everything.

love, i could never hate you. my body would never be at peace with that. it's not that i don't like you. i just can't wrap around the idea of impulse and how quickly everything can change even with agreement to fight otherwise. we grow daily with fate's time, and even though investments are worth gold, we still get betrayed by the illusion that it will never be solid. we even convince ourselves and conform to the idea that time is a passing moment, rather than this fluid-eternal motion of recycled events served as new air, but time lacks compassion so we lose anyway.

where does it go?

no, i don't hate you, nor do i blame you for making adjustment for a life with diligent passing. i gave you space though easy would never be the word for it. my world crumbled in conflict and i had no desire to make you feel the pain of walls closing so i left. i am no stranger to war but you've seen chaos and you didn't deserve that. not from me anyway. i don't know where our friendship is right now and that's all good— i know one thing. i made a vow to respect you and that's a promise i intend to keep.

always.

sunflower:

i literally just took a breath of relief. i told myself i would attempt one last time to see where things are, and you didn't need to explain. i just wanted to hear from you. you've been through enough. i'm just happy i got to see a bit of light from your eyes again.

you deserve a world, i hope you know that.

is it possible for you to ever leave me without trace? i can't tell whether it would hurt less, or cause my fist to fight at the heart more.

her ode summer, *to him.*

to the man i fell in love with,

don't think i ever forgot. we were one of the greatest.

to the man i fell in love with, i was ripped away from you. then you, further, from me. but i'm coming back.

i want to know why i was thrown into this love and what it was meant to teach me.

to the man i fell in love with,

i still stalk you everyday. i caught myself in the act and i decided that i'd end up here... in your messages tonight.

i miss your words bouncing off the walls of my mind.

i miss trying to envision what you look like when you'd speak to me.

i miss that smile... that laugh.

that kiss you'd send me when i needed it.

our plans. our time.

our summer.

that was our summer.

no other man has done what you've done to me.

call me sprung or in love,

i don't think i'll ever give a damn.

i almost feel pathetic though not knowing if i should.

to the man i fell in love with,

i'm sorry.

sorry that so much has come between you and me.

i think of you and i can't help but think about how you are/were all i want/ed.

hours away from america and you're who i wanted to talk to. you made me feel comfortable.

to the man i fell in love with.

i know that being so distant has caused a lot of damage. and i'm not saying that i will be able to just

change things in an instant, but if we can begin at a
crawl back to this, i'd be more than glad to.

and if you need time to think about it,

i can give you that too.

— sunflower

i had a dream last night. i was so eager to steal
something that had already belonged to me. for good
reason i made a connection with you. i try so hard to
keep you and you are already here. i fight for things,
like your attention when i already have it. i just have
to open my soul enough to see and appreciate it for
what it is. i'm not saying that my dream solves
anything as far as the issues we have but it gave me
insight. a hue of understanding how people can stand
together at peace. i went to church two weeks ago,
and when the speaker took podium i remember he
said something like, 'a frame is an important part of a
picture. you put the wrong frame on a photograph
and it cheats the eye of possibility in perception of
things.'

it just made sense to me now. we dissect situations under scope of the wrong frames.

no wonder why time isn't in favor of us, *but we are okay.*

to become revolutionary you must first destroy. tear down and go back to the basics. we have to step back and be reminded of what we were to appreciate who we are in the moment, and accept where we've been. i don't know, maybe i'm babbling like usual but if it resonates at all, reach back.

mo' better blues: a memoir

the arguments became repetitive, often came in form of anger but diffused into passion and love-making. we didn't sleep much. conversation evolved into dependency while dreams distorted the nature of what we both had asked for. i understood she loved me, and no denying i felt that my bones would concur but things got heavy for the both of us. she needed space but failed to speak and i needed her. far more than pride ever allowed me to concede, but in-between silence, we lost it all.

our separation was severe. ego hung by the throat for honesty to come home but it was too late. we built walls to save face to the public, i think we lost this one. she missed me. i felt it.

i missed her. she knew better but time said different. months passed and we found ourselves engaged in subliminal/cyber-stalker-ish activity but we conquered. she called me one night to ask me if she ever came across.

i told her, 'you haunt everything i have come to know but somehow it makes you feel closer than not being here and i'd settle for that.' she smiled. i always knew when she celebrated my existence in laughter, no denying we reached further than most and that…was greater than anything i had ever experienced.

i believe people build in segments, especially in progressing with love. whether new, old, or indifferent. the journey is pivotal. i came to see how closed off i can be sometimes even when i'm open to thought.

trust is not an issue but an anxiety. love knows no distance if your soul can still feel.

i felt hers. i don't know if that was an excuse to see her leave or my closure for it not to hurt so much. regardless, it brought comfort and i came to realize that a lot can disappear in night. no longer oblivious to why people insist on creating memories with anything strong enough to grab you. those moments become your rescue later.

it was freedom to be kissed by a deity. understand why i can never settle for anything less than the moon.

i have been to the mountain top. nothing comes close to falling in a place where gravity is non-existent, and a heart is still free to float in a mass enfolded as the universe. a black hole in constant pull for things accustomed for curiosity and the ache for truth.

molded by animal instincts, i didn't think much when it came to her.

i have no shame in admitting i had it bad. ignorance or convinction, i believed god wrote us in parallel when he thought of communion. we met completely out of order, came close to breaking the chaos theory. left half crazy and a quarter foolish trying to preserve what was meant to teach rather mistaken for a lifetime. i'm not certain about things anymore but i know this to be true. the universe has a funny way of getting away with stuff and we let her.

things i learned:

i. distance amplifies wanting but it cannot recreate itself. people have to.

ii. never forget those who touched places other people been afraid to explore, and remember those who have been there.

iii. allow the sun to kiss you in the morning. a lover somewhere sent the light of day. get wrapped in the feeling. love is only returned when you accept it as a gift.

iv. you can't be everyone's hero. save yourself from the pain of feeling for everyone else.

v.   distance is an illusion, a conviction of the mind.
      what you feel close, is. and what isn't is non-
      existent to your interpretation of what is real.

vi.   love is a nomad. a wanderer. boundless, but it is
      a feeling. a spill of two hearts making love in
      rebirth of a new breath.

vii. arguments can excite and destroy things at the
      same time.

viii. waiting and patience are two different things.

ix.   if given the chance, travel the world and make
      love in every place you touch.

x.   some people will never fade from you. that is not
      always a bad thing.

a blues for niah.

you were a mystery i was drawn into.

something about the way your eyelashes pointed
upwards made me believe that hope still floated
behind eyelids. you…excited me, love.

in the mornings.

i liked the idea of being able to kiss you before the
sun did but who's to blame for the fall.

you made the moon insecure. first conversation our
minds met.

voice. covered in accents dipped in good laughs, i felt
in heaven with you.

far from question, we lost it. morals thrown off, we
sinned ungodly, but every morning felt like prayer.

and every night felt like answers to everything we'd
ever prayed for. you were worth every sin.

ain't no fighting it. i couldn't fight you.

you never fought me.

in time love was lit, passed in rotation.

it happened too fast. it scared you. i know.

but there we were.

a new feel. same rhytm. old heart.

your voice reminded me of— god.

the good things.

a painter in my last lifetime, i remember now.

obsessed with trying to paintbrush your beauty on
canvas with no stroke that ever mastered it.

drunk off colors, your eyelids gave peace to my quiet
place.

in this life, a poet. and you, a lover of words, you
entice me in metaphors.

gave goose bumps in electric shocks like passion
when plugged to the sun. a rush of adrenaline poured
in doses of cracked skin, i got this high for you.

the first woman who ever made my hands tremble.
made curiosity touch places they had never been.

i remember the first time you tried to pronounce my
name: you hesitated, but something about the way
your mouth formed... i'm sorry we didn't work but i
still want to travel the world and make love in every
country with you.

every time you speak of us, the previous us. my mind takes a trip to what it felt like in that experience and what i had missed.

i'm not letting go.

you taught me how to decipher emotion and none of this feels finished yet.

— sunflower

text // eleven: seventeen, *a.m.*

sunflower:

that feeling. that's the feeling right there. i've never
been able to describe it as such, but that's what you
gave me. i expect every guy to be like you and they
aren't— that has made my love life unfortunate lately.
for a moment i started to believe that even you
weren't like you anymore. i just want us to work but i
want it to come natural.

M.

i can say the same. unconsciously i search. search
parts of you in women i meet now but none have
come close to anything we had learned to survive. you
crept inside everything. we gave bone structure and
fell in compliance— i don't know if i'll ever find you,
but we've already lost. now i'm learning to break and
stay in one place at the same time.

i admire you.

thank you for the simple fact that you saw me.

really, saw me.

art is the soul's extension.

PART III

Y ou ever lost yourself/disappeared so much that you forgot who you were and had to rebuild? it's like i'm reintroducing myself to everyone around me but meeting myself for the first time.

— *a question that woke me.*

there is a lot to learn in being disconnected, even prior to the realization of being lost. nothing is indubitably absent—the moment you catch speed with location, you elude the position of where you found yourself *lost*. therefore, absence is juxtaposition. you are everything in every place you remember for the simple fact that you've always known. there has always been a depth to your existence. whenever you introduce yourself to new people, it may feel like you're shaking your own hand for the first time. you are visiting an old place and maybe that is the magic of a soul wanderer. you realize that you are new. you've shed old skin and matured into being. so next time you rotate into thought, accept your disappearance as holy; allow balance to serve nutrition and nurture this new body experience.

be your own best friend. it will get lonely sometimes but solitude is necessary. and though separation models growth, understand the human connection is a milestone for evolution. find equilibrium, shake those hands, introduce yourself to the universe. you are new, and old, familiar and *here*— because you've always been.

i don't want to be your friend only, but again, acceptance— i can try. i don't wish to battle myself…that battle can never proclaim a winner. i don't want to stand alone in love, but if friendship is what you wish, then i have to accept.

i'm here. i would rather be *here*, there with you, in friendship than to dispose of you.

real.

— woman who loved *boy.*

have you ever been nervous when speaking to a
beautiful girl?

have you ever been nervous standing nakedly in front
of a beautiful woman?

imperfections become apparent

weakness within words, open.

not knowing what she was thinking…and

how did you feel when she first touched you?

that's how i feel about showing my poems to
someone like you.

— the woman who wanted to share poems.

confessions:

i need to hit a point where vulnerability becomes second nature. i give it too much power because i believe if i open up to people...well just that. i don't want to lose my gold i suppose. is that selfish?

a bit selfish if you've got a heaven to offer.

i've missed you my whole life.

> then tell me everything
> you've always wanted
> to say.

i'm a big clutter of chaos and disorder. vulnerability isn't really my thing, but somehow i'm okay with it when it comes to you. i love how alive it makes me feel. i could cry. i've been reading schopenhauer a lot lately. there is a passage where he talks about being that i love and it reminds me of you. basically he explains, i, as an individual, will come to an end with my death. but my individuality is not my essential and ultimate being, only a manifestation of it. my individuality is not the thing itself but only a phenomenal form of which appears under the aspect of time and consequently, has a beginning nor end, nor the bounds of a given individuality. thus no individuality can exclude it.

it exists in everyone, everywhere.

in the former sense, therefore, i will when i die become nothing. in the latter— everything. i think loving you is a lot like being dead. there's this threshold i've transcended. i do not wish to come back, and i'll continue to *feel* as long as you don't leave me.

you are the most dangerous thing that i have felt but
have never touched.

come dance with me.

your physical, not your spirit this time.

she was born out of water with rain underneath her tongue praying for god to open air for the clouds in her mouth.

.

ACT III: FORBIDDEN FRUITS

'i never thought it was possible to fall in love with
two people at the same time' he thought.

K ai was an angel. she had to be, she said
things that made hearts drop but for as long
as i knew her, she was a light source. a
powerhouse with motion careful not to
shatter a heart. i never understood but that's
who she was. a channel. everything drifted in
her direction. some days you could hear the wind
crying when she passed. i was convinced that
earthquakes were ancestors underneath her feet
tugging in turbulence asking to be loved a bit more.
her energy was surreal.

'why are you naked' she would ask on days i forgot to
wear a smile outside a rectangle of a colored door. it
got me. a quiet laugh would creep in the base of my

throat because i had a thing for the sun and our relationship was no secret. kai was not foreign to the thought.

'i had a dream last night.'

'about what' i asked, curious as usual.

'butterflies— color, wings, everything' she said. 'i was being reincarnated into one. fighting transition, flashes of life all directed to you. awkwardly your smile helped ease the transfer, it made me feel safe— strange. i found myself drawn somehow.'

right before her mouth closed, she looked at me with a soft in her eyes, 'stop invading my dreams, dude.' we laughed.

she was curious. i could tell by the way her fingertips aligned with my shoulder blades in search for reassurance, and i understood. sometimes you have to pinch whatever is close to wake up from a dream. i was odd with the things i paid attention to.

kai was a smooth girl. silver-tongued but not one to convince that she knew everything. humble, certainly not a stranger to being taught and i liked that about her.

'you talk to the missus yet?' kai asked every morning
to validate her theory on the types of men she
thought succeeded in a heart's chase. she always
found me with a shoulder shrug.

'you funny. that ain't my girl.'

'the way you watch her she might as well be.' tugging
at my arm. we laughed with no concern for the world.
watching her smile was a luxury. kai was chaotic but a
fusion of good merit so we made it work.

kayla. let me tell you about this deity.

she was the type to break hearts, but i too, would run
her bath water if the bid ever came.

okay, maybe not all that but kayla was a goddess of a
woman. her presence carried a current when she
walked. stood in essence that made my blood clog
with insecurity— quiet in my own pulse, i was
breathing composure inside my skin. i admired her
grace to just be. she understood control and
everybody wanted to know about her. self-awareness
is lethal for anyone who understands power. the

cadence of quiet energy and the secret of evolution allows people to fall in love with unsolved mystery. she understood, what you feed— you become.

every intake affects the water inside your body, and balance is essential for those who soul travel. equilibrium is the heart of a spiritual journey. our existence is orchestrated through blood infused with energy serving as holding blocks for external connections; like breathing. it's the nature of all things. the universe is an open space of imagination that of a child. our bodies were designed to explore same.

we learn in increments. you come to find that any space you allow yourself to be seen completely naked, is the purest form of untampered energy. the math you come open to is not found in numbers anymore, you find it in self-preservation. i prayed that my instincts were right about her.

'hi...' she said, walking past my books in the library. her smile did not visit often but something lit up. i think my life made sense in that moment.

'kayla...right?' i pretended not to know her name

while both arms reached. each bone in my body conspired movement with muscle to make this encounter prominent. handshake firm, but gentle.

no stutters or second thoughts. our energy kissed, i felt a pulse connect and my knees buckled. i could feel blood coursing miles across this galaxy of a body in celebration of nature's law. this travel called for a feast in my skin and i was consumed.

'yes, kayla.' she smiled again. look at god!

serendipity.

kai walked over to the open space and sat across the table from us —unnoticed, she cleared her throat and claimed a portion of the territory.

'hi, i'm kai. his conscience, the other half that he lost.' i was never proper at introductions and women i fall for have a way of making my stomach feeble— anemic so i froze. tongue-tied in question, they both looked past my shoulders and caved into laughs. i was the clown at the party.

'i'm kayla, nice to meet you.' she extended an arm.

it's easier to dodge bullets when you see the gun pulled but it was too late. the chemistry kicked off, the ambiance was created by gods. palm sweating. marathons. silence, there was a peace internal.

i was walking in my sleep that even time started to breathe. caught in the crossfire, i was a glitch in a dream which i desperately needed to run from. kai was my best friend, and kayla— well, she was girl i just met. what was i thinking? emotions unparalleled to thought and honestly, i had no desire to fix this lack of resistance when it came to the heart of them.

you never know how adjacent love is until a stranger brings you closer to that truth. only now it's a triangle. two days passed since the trinity formed and kai was being distant again. i was uncertain to why she felt the need for space but her absence started to drag on me.

in uncertainty, you come to realize that 'presence' is often taken for a causal gesture. we have no idea how much we care for people until time creates a war against everything we have allowed to settle as routine.

'i miss you. reach when you can, i need help with that

math homework.' i texted her. silently, she became ghost. a distant memory that i wanted to remember but even certainty is a luxury only time can offer so i waited.

kayla and i were good, getting to know her felt familiar. a distant yet delicate memory she was dream in reverse. we found rhythm and acquired a taste in the energy of passing moments, i had to remind myself to breathe around her. she nurtured heaven, space only marked for kings to have named me one. our company was no overcast, each conversation carried weight— hungry to be fed, our minds became a new recipe for rebellion. we just wanted to live. she initiated change and however far, i do not remember the last time i wanted to kiss a mind in revolution but her thoughts were suitable. i wanted to read more, not just books but indulge in the elaborate nature of all things.

when you make love to complexity, everything simple fights to be understood under the notion of all or nothing. if ever you come close to who you really are, an extension or solely an experience in connection to another being; relish yourself in that energy. find some freedom in your luck because nothing matters as the weight of a moment. as i spent time with kayla i discovered an ancient secret and i wanted to flaunt it. life is simple— and moments are imperative. the moment you experience a pattern in which your nose fluctuates when taking up new air is the moment breathing becomes more than just routine for staying alive. i decided to be present and allow every moment to mean something. people have the tendency to reach too far in oblivion and forget that earth is heavy. they forge expectations which never live past the assumption we already have for the world.

i would rather like things for what they are, and slowly i began to. life is funny that way; you form beliefs and they mold reason around things you already think are important to you. in light of this revelation, i became a walking contradiction in my own belief that moments— are people just breathing through time. what happens when you lose the two?

i know i was losing a friend in chase of another.

time evolved and nothing came. i'm used to knocks at my window at 2 a.m. for city escapades and diner cravings but— *nothing*. something had to be wrong, kai. i came to understand she was the type to repel at any moment when she felt uneasy. you know, the kind who needed to understand the boundary of her own space before sharing perimeter. space isn't to be given just to anyone and things felt different after knowing that.

three days later, she knocked at my door in red lipstick, a color she never wore. she never wore make-up period. her body enfolded in a dress that kissed fabric at every corner my eyes could not resist. she stared at me with eyebrows arched and heels above ground. i haven't seen her dress expensive since sunday school. and even then, it was never done by choice. mama shakur never played about her church clothes, kai knew better than to twist her nerves on a sunday morning. everything was different about her.

'where have you been?' i asked anxious, overwhelmed with curiosity.

she did not say much. she just stared and smiled like usual.

'you ready?' she asked.

'ready for…' she lost me.

things were different. i couldn't decode the excitement or justify why she felt her approach was okay for reunion. i find mystery as a go-to-trait most women dabble into when inclined to mind games. i know a woman can ask for space and say *i miss you* in the same breath, though i never really understood that. kai was spontaneous, i could never tell with this girl but i admired her audacity to explore things unguardedly. she would say, 'moments are meant to be lived not waited for and when learning patience, remember to reach for things you also feel you deserve.'

'you always want to know everything, why?' she smiled. 'come on, get dressed.' she insisted by pulling the side of my shirt making her way through the door. i never questioned her motives and time never really gave me a reason to. parts of me missed her too much to fetch for answers. her presence served a better escape; i got to lose myself in the magic again. moments are vital for me now, and when you find yourself in company of warming spirits don't chase your mind for what happens next. trust the night to kiss you just long enough to feel the hues, relax.

i heard marvin gaye playing in the living room as i was getting dressed but to no surprise, our hearts had grown out of a speaker box. the radio was a poor man's invention with a sprinkle of soul food when tongues grew empty next to dinner plates. we lived in a middle class neighborhood and police sirens. heard everything from morning traffic to neighbors fighting and nothing got past us. nobody could afford thicker walls, but we lived. survived off secondhand conversations and communal strength. as you get older, you realize what weight childhood must've been for you. exposed early to adult conversations and curiosity stuck to the roof of unheard prayers, but it made you pay more attention.

kai was a fan. even at nine coming from school, she would listen to motown and jazz records her mom would leave unplaced around the blue house on 5th street.

i never understood the correlation between jazz and children who had to grow so young, but it was worth sight.

i was unsure of what to wear to complement the black in her dress, it gave good posture to her physique but i think i did well. white-buttoned shirt pressed neatly and khaki jeans that made me look a lot taller than i was. 'you look handsome. i could almost date you.' she laughed. i could never tell if her jokes aligned with any truth but i know she meant well.

walking out the door, things felt right again. and though i still wondered of her whereabouts. none of it mattered. she was here. i wouldn't dare ruin this ambiance with honesty. i took a few breaths before i broke the silence with a question i half wanted an answer to.

'...where we going?'

'you'll see. give me your keys, i'll drive this time.' she said as her palm extended. i wanted to hold her hand but i knew better, the tension was too close to home to play with fire in absence of emergency exits.

(crossroads.)

i'm at war fighting two sides with absent morals.

here— falling for my best friend with a double sword and conflict pulling the heart in different directions.

i was learning the core value of friendship and i couldn't afford any mishaps. not with kai.

'we're here,' she said softly, parking as her face gave home to new dimples; another weakness i had to build resistance for. she had a glow i hadn't seen in a while and light was the best element to her existence. the line was packed, overcrowded with people but we walked in as if we owned the place. i told you kai had a magic to her, only she was able to pull strings like that.

the atmosphere was calm, jazzy nothing overdressed. a moment of epiphany; i realized that time with her felt a lot like a dream. i was happy to know that my best friend knew exactly what my soul looked like— it was the only way that she was able to bring me to such a place. i celebrated that.

she made dinner reservations at la grassa, an italian lounge serving pizza, bread, poetry serenaded by jazz musicians. she knew heaven's recipe. my heart was on the floor crawling to whatever she had to give.

'show me.' awkward, i was put me on the spot again.

'what?' looking around i laughed with a nervous in my throat.

'don't play dumb, you know exactly what i want.' she pointed to the stage.

'poetry. you still got it?'

i couldn't say no.

walking to the stage earthquakes caught up with my feet. i despised attention, i hated lights. eyes made me nervous and it wasn't the crowd— it was kai but i didn't expect her to know any this. she's never put me on the spot before. you would think that words which come with the flow of water would be easy to spill for someone you thought deserved life and all its memories, but there i was. stuck, eyes closed, standing nervous then suddenly— *rain.*

'i wanted to meet your voice half way.

hold hands in chaos and kiss in vibration, mix—

your mouth with earthquakes, i wanted every reason
to kiss until your soul came.

escape in the pores of your skin. feel your back
arched with hands still in tune with prayer.

forgive me with a door closed. woman.

i wanted to touch your lips, anxious. trace your
insides with white residue

[- - - -] some sense out of you.'

silence.

before i knew it, i was transported to a different
world. a place where passion didn't bother to save
face with words understood like the back of a hand.
kai was on her feet before the poem finished. i've
never seen her anxious to get to anyone. she started
walking toward me clapping. it was an honor. she
came running in reach for a hug and as i stretched, i
felt a heart trying to catch up with breathing patterns.
'i didn't know you had it in you. maybe i

underestimate.' she played it off head tilted barely looking my way.

'i'm all right,' i said confidently playing it cool. we laughed as usual but this time it was different, the night changed. we were closer than two friends taking part of good energy and familiar space, we didn't pretend.

'it's getting late. let's go home,' she smiled.

i didn't realize how much time had passed. 'let me drive,' i laughed mocking movements with my hand. 'you drive like someone tip-toeing on a third strike.' we laughed again then slowly pulled off in the quiet of the night. the drive home reassured everything. things had always felt easy with kai. even in absence of words her silence was never empty and i admired that.

as cars passed, i noticed a reflection in her smile. no seriously, the moon bounced off her pupils; crescent in shape, it reflected exactly what her mouth formed. she reached over slowly and brushed her hand against mine. what a feeling, warmth. certainty. magic, something i haven't felt in a while. she traced her fingers across my veins as if drawn to places my blood flowed. vibrant, she raised curiosity to the bone, i could feel my skin form into goose bumps. slowly, she turned my hand. stared at my palm as if she was trying to make room for herself in my lifelines. i smiled.

'what do you see?' i asked trying to push my luck. she stopped.

'your nails are dirty,' she laughed but i just looked at her.

'don't be a baby. i'm only kidding—your life is long. i heard once that if you put two hands together the course of their lives change. you share it. pain is not just yours anymore and happiness is amplified if the palms align. so, here i go searching for truth again.' she smiled a lot more than a glass full, i swear time stopped. i started to feel things in my chest for her. perhaps imagined, i drove at the lowest speed possible trying to savor this moment because tomorrow may not always fall in my favor. the anxiety was thick, heavy that a knife would cut the tension with ease through barbed wire. we wanted to feel things.

it was quiet the rest of the way. i pulled over two

houses down from where she lived because i needed answers. silent.

'where've you been?'

'here,' she answered calmly.

'i been here… always, with you. it might seem i created distance but i wanted you to see me. i wanted you to reach.'

'i did.'

'you think you did, but you didn't.'

she looked at me painful. i felt *shallow*— flightless and unsure, it was best to listen as her mouth moved in search for the right words to spill.

'silence is an open invitation to show effort. i wanted you to look for me. i know how you feel about distance but you didn't have to give up on my silence. i wanted you to fight a little; show me that i was worth any anger— one that came out of love because i mattered to you that much. i wanted my absence to mean something.'

at this moment, it was light to assume what she felt

for me. i reached over her arm and brought her closer.

'i do see you. i'm here— i've always been.'

static. my words were gentle, but raw. i wanted her to pick up on my urgency to convince that she mattered that much, because she did.

'thank you for tonight.' she kissed me.

'always.' i replied. she slammed the door before i could say another word and the night was gone.

i never looked at kai this way but black dresses with red lipstick started to grow on me. i was falling in love with my best friend.

it is easier to date your best friend most people would say; i never thought i would find myself in a predicament where i would ever weigh that as an option. i convinced myself i wouldn't dare lose a friendship in pursuit of something bigger than what i had enough mechanism to nurture— but life is sick like that. i figured quickly sacrifice works in two ways. you either chase to lose, or you lose refusing to chase possibility and both require faith.

i was supposed to hang out with kayla after school the next day, but i couldn't wrap things that i felt with kai. the energy was too real to shake off. i wanted to understand. not just for my sake but for the three of us. is it possible to fall in love with two people at the same time?

no answer.

do you believe in serendipity? some call it fate. those who fall short of moderate judgment refer to that magic as fortune or a crack in god's whisper, but do you believe in anything?

i believe in a woman. i believe fools can fall in love and nobody understands the verdict when bodies fall outside of things they know— but we rush for the hunt so we chase anyway. i believe people are good at writing, others paint better what they convince themselves to be real, but neither the painter, nor the writer understands the weight of this transfer fully. the space between curiosity and understanding but they both try. they believe in something. those who've been to the moon may say that i'm naïve about love, but i'm not stupid to recognize when my soul is being

kissed with conviction to breathe for someone. the
moments i spent with kai, my spirit was dancing.

the days i made love to kayla heaven could write itself
in spirit of tongue, but where did my morals go?

ACT IV: SOUL WIND

note to self.

now that you have exposed your doubts to the universe, it is ready to fight. keep you at the mercy of your own judgment, but this is what had to be done. nothing aligns without friction. your life is a testament to wars and oversight. you fall short, you learn, you grow. you live.

transparency is camouflage.

but breathe,

you are okay.

— **prophecy.**

life is too short to pretend you have everything figured out. you must be confident in your ability to learn and exercise patience, then teach bystanders things you have come to know. a simple gesture keeps a soul alive. ask to be fed. give more than you ask. acquire freedom when you live this way.

i have spent a good portion of my life chasing things, waiting. waiting for them to happen. waiting for people to happen. created a necessity rather than prepare for them. i was wrong to live my life like that. never again.

if ever you find a woman who resembles poetry.
head-wrapped in metaphors— heart warm like
morning coffee, do not hesitate. ask for a lifetime.
spend it unapologetically.

inhale the universe inside her skin.

this is *home*.

a passionate woman is worth the chaos.

what you love, you lose at least once.

the woman who traced my jawline.

i like her. the space is warm. winter is non-existent
when her mind is a place i could sleep in every night.

her mouth is a revolution with a scratch table for a
heart. she speaks of renaissance. order. we breathe in
intimacy.

fingertips trace jawlines and tongues move in secret of
open apartments. drawn. the heart is usually quiet but
moans trigger time bombs i have no desire to stop.
explosions have became a second home.

how dare you not like it here? she likes me. the shiver
in our voice can't be fought with resistance anymore,

instead, we kiss earthquakes with turbulence built
inside our bones in light of winter, no hesitance—

it's just us.

she kissed me again.

hands are intimate,

couches breathe.

time is a remix.

bodies teach.

voice is heavy.

mind is portal.

touch is human.

pinky promises can be broken by a kiss.

we cheat ourselves.

love is liquid.

god is womb.

space is infinite.

water is deep.

eyes are foreplay.

[fo(r]e)play.

be careful who you share your space with. do not
sleep with the devil and expect to wake up in heaven
draped in white sheets, at the service of wine bottles.

— **sandcastle**

attachment is a disease. let go of everything you are afraid to lose, then reconnect without commitment as a blanket for dependency.

b e n e d i c t i o n.

one day,

i will look at a woman and everything in my stomach
will turn. the turbulence of everything i feel will be
pushed through my ribcage and project on my tongue
with humble gratitude for the gift of sharing space
with a sacred being.

a deity. a garden flower disguised in flesh of a woman
for soul purpose.

her aura will be magnetic. her silhouette unmatched-
celestial perhaps one third god with heaven for
eyelids.

i will be lucky.

my skin will be an open window with soul magnets
that reflect attraction and love particles. we will be
stardust.

two forces pulled from different directions of fatal attraction and combust into flames of unheard prayers and gravity falls.

love is a journey. a union is an alliance. a spirited signature of fighting for more.

and one day, i will look at you:

teach the boy that forgot to pray.

hold the hand that forgot to give.

feed the mind afraid to commit.

give freedom in all i forgot,

i will be consumed by fire and celebrate the beauty of the morning. the sound of cars passing, red salvia draped by the window next to her favorite paintings.

i will write of collarbones in a favorite notebook.

black—

is a bold color to spill ink with somebody's name
smeared in god's tears.

eternal residue.

i will wear it proudly. tongue tied, i will speak of her.
the way she looks at me with hands ready to dance
across insecurities and a new life.

i will live on her tongue with life written in brail inside
a mouth only a lover can understand, and this—

this will be *home.*

you can be fire, and water, and coexist with wind all in the same.

ABOUT THE AUTHOR

Malanda Jean-Claude Kisongo is an artist, a writer who believes creativity fuels true happiness. Deems vulnerability as holy and finds any medium to express that sentiment as a symbol for peace.

Twitter: @overlyxclusive

Instagram: elusivemetaphors

Website: www.ogjean.com